# Pretty Pops

## ADVENTURES:

### DAVID'S SPECIAL STAR

Written by
**Dr. Andrea**

Illustrations by
**Titan Fahmi**

AC
**An Imprint of AC Publishing Ltd**

For my beloved nephews Reggie Webster, Wesley Webster and Lil Russell Webster. You will always be my special stars.

www.prettypopsworld.com
ISBN: 978-1-957-08025-3
Cover designed by: Titan Fahmi

Once upon a time in Dinosaurland, lived a young Afrovenator Dinosaur named David. He had a loving family, but something was missing.

Meet David, the Afrovenator,
Pretty Pops' friend.

Him and his Dad, Charlie would hunt meat.

Every night Mama, Dad and
David would sit down to eat.

"Pretty Pops, why can't I see my Dad? Is he far?"

"David, my Granny said that your Dad lives in the stars."

Pretty Pops said, "David my Granny said that when someone we love goes away, they go up about this high, and become a special star in the night sky. They shine down on us keeping us safe and sound."

David points to the sky. "Do you think that's my Dad's star, Pretty Pops?"

Pretty Pops points to the sky and says, "Yes, David! That bright one shining down on us is his."

"I want to be just like Dad one day," David said. Pretty Pops replied, "Oh you are much like him. More than you know."

David's Dad was a famous baseball player. David started to practice baseball like his dad used to do.

"Go, David, go!" David's friends were cheering him on at his baseball game.

"You play so much like your Dad," Mom said.

"You're becoming just like your dad each day David," said Pretty Pops.

"Look, Dad, we're having a picnic just like you used to," said David.

"Mom, I'm going to write a letter to Dad, do you think he will see it?" asked David.

"You bet he will," Mom said.
"I'm proud of you, David," said
Mom.

Dad, my guide, a shining light, He's up there with the moon, in the starry night. My tears may fall like gentle rain, my memory of him will always remain. The warm hugs, the stories shared, are treasures in my heart, declared.

In every twinkle of the night, his love
still glows so pure and bright.
So, I embrace the love he gave, Hold
on to memories, strong and brave.
For though he's gone, he's never far.
In every twinkle, like a shining star.

Mom said, "Even though Dad is
no longer here...

He shines bright in your heart just like his special star in the night sky, my Dear."

"Goodnight, Dad. I love you."

www.ingramcontent.com/pod-product-compliance
Lightning Source LLC
Chambersburg PA
CBHW041800040426
42447CB00001B/39